Just Me Now

Just Me Now

The First Year of Life
without My Spouse

Vic Harrison

Cover Design, Editing, and Formatting by DanelleYoung.com
Proofreading by JamisWords.com

Just Me Now / Vic Harrison
ISBN: 979-8-9910960-0-3 (Paperback)
ISBN: 979-8-9910960-1-0 (eBook)
Library of Congress Control Number: 2024917812

Praise be to . . . the God of all comfort, who comforts us in all our troubles, so that we can comfort those in any trouble with the comfort we ourselves receive from God.

2 Corinthians 1:3–4

Contents

Introduction

Many people all around us are dealing with the loss of a beloved spouse. Each person and each experience is unique. While no two situations can be exactly alike, there may be some aspects that are quite common for all who have lost their husband or wife, especially for those who are widowed at an all-too-early age. I understand that some have suffered from their loss far more than I have, and I know some who have struggled far less. Whether due to unexpected, sudden events or due to protracted illness, there seems to be no best or easy way to let go of your loved one. Each loss has its challenges.

Likewise, the amount of time spent in grief can differ for people. There's no prescribed duration. But most things do change over time, and only time can give us a better perspective on all the events. In some regards, I will always feel the same about my spouse as I do today, but in other respects, there may be a progression and a change over time. Certainly, we all hope we'll eventually make progress in dealing with our loss. And there is undoubtedly a continuum of "healthy" grief that will allow us to mend somewhat as we go along. The expressed purpose of this book is to focus on the first year of my grief. Still, I am keenly aware that my perspective will be different two years, five years, and ten years down the road than it is in this early period. Admittedly, my perspective after eight months was different than my perspective at three months after my wife's death. The observations and thoughts recorded here come from a relatively early period in the process.

The chapters in this book will
1. describe my wife, Ruth Harrison;
2. briefly detail the sickness she went through;
3. attempt to relate what the experience has been like for me during this first year without her;
4. describe the role faith has played; and
5. list the steps I have been taking thus far to cope with my loss.

The purpose of this work is threefold:
1. To be a means for me to think through and process my grief
2. To attempt to explain to family and friends what I've been going through
3. To let other widows and widowers know they aren't alone on this lonely road

Ruth grew up attending a large church with a strong music ministry. The music minister was influential and cared about the congregation. Under his leadership, Ruth began to use her musical gifts. She was so influenced through the years by this man that, as a teenager, she prayed she would someday marry a music minister. I happened to be the volunteer music minister at my home church when I first met Ruth. At the time, I was seriously considering attending seminary and becoming a full-time vocational music minister.

Jump ahead ten months, and we were married—that's ten months after our first date.

A few months after our wedding, I accepted my first paid music ministry position. The following year, we moved to Louisville to attend seminary. I maintained my part-time position at our small rural church. We would drive back on the weekends for services and activities. Ruth's prayer for a music minister husband had been answered. (And my prayers were answered, too, by the way!)

After a couple of years in that situation, we spent the next twelve years in full-time ministry in two locations. After that, I spent over twenty years teaching public school music. Ruth also began her career as a music teacher but shifted to special education after four years. While we were educators, we ministered together as co-Bible study leaders in our local church. We did that for many years. Whether in full-time ministry, teaching, or lay-leadership, Ruth was beside me every step of the way, and that is the hallmark of our story.

Ruth at our apartment in Louisville, Kentucky

1

The Woman She Was

Before talking about the year after my wife passed, I'll share some of Ruth's background. One year later, it's still difficult to talk about her in the past tense. The memories are so fresh, and I continue to relive so many moments. Sometimes, it's as if she is still here even though she's not. "Was?" That's a complex concept to grasp, though my mind knows she is gone. She was and still is precious to me.

Ruth's background will give an indication of how far she fell due to her disease. Any loving husband surely has great things to say about his late wife, and I am no exception. I could fill many pages with the positives of her life—her influence on me and on others. She wasn't perfect by any means (nor am I). Our marriage wasn't perfect either, though it was great.

First, here are some thoughts that came from other people. Before her death, I sought ways to help Ruth and me deal with the difficulties we were facing. I asked our Bible study class to describe Ruth in one word or tell me what Ruth was known for. These are some common answers:

uplifting energetic *gift of hospitality*
fun joyful *zest for life*
kind *genuine* witty
funny humorous *hilarious* warmth
her smile
love for people goofy *pure joy*
laugh
lighting up a room with love and laughter
positive big curly hair
energy musical talent unwavering
making faith
everyone *beautiful voice*
feel welcome living for Christ

These words came directly from our class members without any embellishment. Ruth was technically my co-teacher for our Bible study class, but she was more than that. She was the glue that held us all together. While I was the primary Bible teacher, Ruth was the one who provided the humor. She kept the class in stitches and went out of her way to sit with, talk with, and make each person feel welcome. My wife enjoyed hosting cookouts, campouts, parties, and open houses. The way she led in our class complemented my teaching.

She exemplified the same traits in her workplace as an elementary teacher. Ruth brought joy and positivity to the halls and classrooms of the schools where she worked. I know because of all the cards I received from her co-workers after Ruth's death. Everyone echoed the same sentiments. At the end of the school year in 2021, Ruth's school, Foust Elementary, established a new annual award to honor her memory. The Ruth Harrison Sunshine Award is presented to a boy and a girl who stand out for making a positive difference in the lives of others during the school year. I was honored to present the first awards to the winners that year.

Ruth was indeed known for her outgoing, positive, uplifting personality. Her history shows how multifaceted she was. She was a gifted athlete in high school, succeeding as a softball, tennis, and basketball player. Her very competitive spirit served her well as a point guard on the basketball team that won a regional championship two years in a row, making it to the Kentucky State Tournament (Sweet 16). During her college years, she excelled as a starting shortstop on the Kentucky Wesleyan softball team. She also became a valuable member of the KWC tennis team and was once voted MVP by a local media outlet. Old letters from coaches and a recent testimony from one coach corroborated she was quite competitive and had an aggressive style of play.

Her competitive nature continued as an adult as she enjoyed tennis, softball, and ping-pong. She dearly loved playing card games and board games with family and friends and took great joy in winning. But win or lose, she always had fun.

Though she was a gifted athlete in college, Ruth majored in music. She was a flute player and an exceptional vocalist. Again, words from someone other than myself affirm her exceptionality. A couple of months after Ruth's funeral, I ran into an academic colleague of mine who had attended college with Ruth. This music teacher is a gifted vocalist in her own right. I also happen to be acquainted with two other fine sopranos from Ruth's college days. And considering the incredible talent they possess, this former classmate of Ruth's, who was now my teaching peer, divulged this information:

"I really did feel she was the best soprano at the college in those days. Her voice seemed so natural and easy for her. I would practice and practice but could never get close to her sound and strength. I told her I wanted to sing like her when I grew up. She didn't like to practice yet still produced unbelievable tone and sound quality."

Therefore, in my years as a music minister, whatever church I was serving in always had this unusually gifted soprano to help the choir, sing solos, or sing duets with me. My wife could also play the piano and accompany me in that way. She was an able ministry partner in each church I served, leading children's choirs and sometimes vacation Bible schools. Additionally, she made it a point to reach out to senior adults and fellowship with them. She was known for her Rook parties and senior trips.

Part of being a vocational minister is being on call all the time. During my ministry years, I led worship and worked with teenagers, senior adults, and families. Many times, I was called away to the hospital or an emergent need. No matter what we were doing or what I missed, Ruth was always supportive and encouraging—never negative. Her attitude, outlook on life, and talents all made her the perfect complement to a music minister's work and life.

Ruth giving a children's sermon at Burlington Baptist

After I left vocational ministry, I served as an interim worship leader for a few years. That took me to other churches, leaving Ruth alone many Sundays to manage our family's morning routine. Ruth always saw that our two boys were ready and in church in my absence. She continued to participate in music ministry at our new church, First Baptist Church of Owensboro. In my absence, she was very active as a soloist, choir member, Sunday school teacher, and vocal ensemble member. During our years together as Sunday school leaders at First Baptist, we again performed solos and duets together in worship.

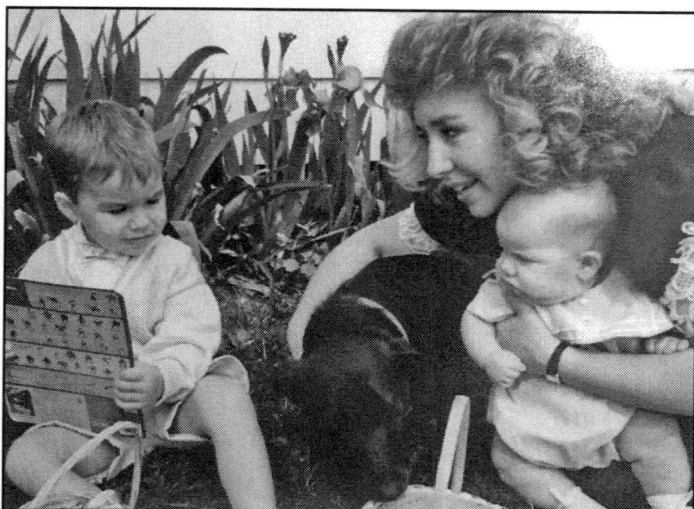

Easter Sunday with our two boys and dog

The complementary nature of her life to mine didn't stop outside of church. We also partnered well at home. Ruth planned and cooked meals while I assisted with cleaning and rearranging furniture for get-togethers. She was well known for great cooking, especially tasty desserts. Outside, there was always a lawn to mow or land to care for. Our lots have ranged in size from half an acre to eleven and a half acres. I like to mow, but she absolutely loved it. We had a one-acre lot for several years and used only a push-type mower to cut the grass. Ruth was our primary lawn worker because she wanted the exercise and loved to do it. Sometimes, we would double up, each pushing a mower, or our two boys would assist. Toward the end of my father's life, he was in poor health. We made the weekly 140-mile round trip for several years to mow and trim his two-acre lawn in Christian County, Kentucky. True to form, Ruth was always there to help and sometimes even did the job herself. At our own homes, Ruth was also the master landscaper and interior decorator. She loved being outside and working in the soil to plant and manage the flowers and shrubs. She also excelled at interior decorating and creating flower arrangements.

About to get her hands dirty

Then there's the matter of our new house. For years, we had taken leisurely drives together through the country, patiently waiting and looking for the potential to have more land and possibly a new home. When the time came, and we found some suitable land, the Lord blessed us with our current eleven and a half acres. I'd heard stories about how difficult and stressful building a new house can be. While considering the mental cost, I didn't feel I had the patience or mindset, even the fortitude, to go through what was required. But Ruth's drive and determination persuaded me to purchase the land and build a house. Though it had been a dream and a prayer of ours, Ruth's drive saw the project through. Though I still played my part, she carried the weight and stress of making most of the decisions. That brings me to who "that woman" was, and is, to me.

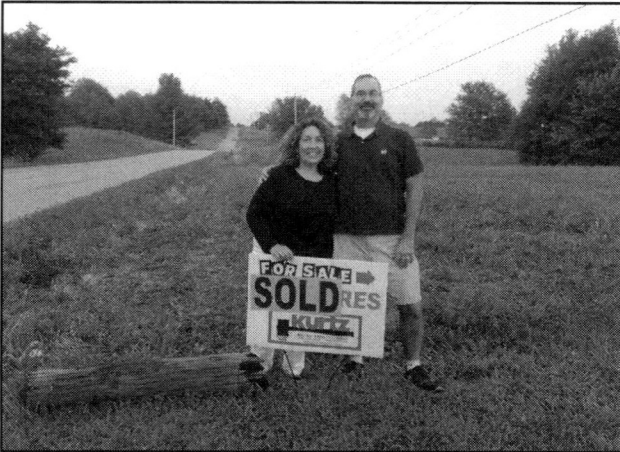

Our new property

Ruth's strong will and ability to make decisions made her my most trusted advisor. That's one of many roles she played in my life. I attempted to make a list.

My wife was
+ my helpmate,
+ lover,
+ supporter,
+ cheerleader,
+ encourager,
+ closest friend,
+ companion,
+ partner,
+ advisor,
+ playmate,
+ counselor,
+ comforter,
+ strengthener,
+ anchor,
+ uplifter,
+ source of confidence,
+ my other half,
+ my better half,
+ sometimes my assistant,
+ sometimes my boss,
+ my cook,
+ sounding board,

+ security blanket,
+ bed-warmer,
+ the one who called me a bed-warmer,
+ a person to bounce thoughts and ideas off of,
+ the one who purchased appropriate clothing for me,
+ the one who helped me dress appropriately,
+ the counterbalance to my reserved and cautious nature,
+ the one who took me to surgeries and medical tests,
+ the one I dropped off at work,
+ the one who dropped me off at work,
+ the one who loved my musical creations the most,
+ the one who picked me up when I was down, and
+ always the positive one.

Since we were both musicians and music continues to play a huge role in my life, I like to think of our marriage in musical terms. We literally and figuratively "made music together" for almost thirty-five years. We were two melodies that possessed beauty on our own. But together, we made even more beautiful harmony. We were partners in many ways and good ones. Only after Ruth's passing did I realize just how unique our relationship was.

Evidence has mounted over the months, as voiced by friends and acquaintances from various walks of life. During the last months of Ruth's illness, there were co-workers from my school who didn't know Ruth well but commented how our relationship seemed to be a model to live by. Others said they hoped to be "loved like that" someday. One of our closest friends told me that Ruth and I had an emotional bond that many couples do not have. After the funeral, others offered similar comments. Nearly one year after her passing, at a church meeting, an acquaintance of ours commented that Ruth and I had a special bond. Yes, we did.

Our last Sunday at Kelly Baptist in Hopkinsville, Kentucky

Our family in 2014

2

The Illness That Changed Our Lives

Ruth Harrison was energetic, physically gifted, active, full of life, and a positive force in every room she entered. Ruth enjoyed every experience. Things began to change, however. And when things started deteriorating, it felt like we were on a one-way street, always going downhill. Somehow, it feels right to couch Ruth's battle with lymphoma, neuropathy, and disability in terms of the experience for both of us. For this is how we dealt with much of life—together. Of course, Ruth was the one who faced the most trauma, suffering, and challenges due to her illness. But it also changed me forever in ways I still seek to understand and deal with as the days go by.

During the 2018 Christmas season, Ruth entertained and hosted several groups in the new house. We had just completed it and moved in the year before. We'd entertained for years in our old place, but this was finally the culmination of her dream—to have a larger space to entertain guests and feed friends. Her gift of hospitality was beaming brightly.

However, during the holidays, she felt like each event took more out of her physically than usual. She was noticeably more tired. She wondered if getting older was the cause. As spring dawned and folks took to preparing the soil for flowers, gardens, and the like, Ruth was doing no less. One day, she went to the home of some church friends to advise them about gardening and to help clean out a flower bed. But after working with them for a short while, she fainted. That was the first warning sign.

Then at school during a normal workweek, she felt faint. The health tech checked Ruth's blood pressure. It was very, very low. At home in our garden, she had another near-fainting episode. Another check of her blood pressure indicated it was extremely low. Visits to our family practitioner, a cardiologist, and a hematologist/oncologist followed.

There was suspicion of a heart problem. An unusual oscillating mass was spotted on one of her heart valves. Yet, we never did get an answer as to what that was. Other health issues became more urgent. Worse yet, a CT scan later revealed many enlarged lymph nodes. A subsequent PET scan ultimately showed the enlarged lymph nodes but also extensive tumor growth all over Ruth's body. It was an extensive case of what a biopsy later confirmed to be diffuse large B-cell lymphoma (a type of non-Hodgkin's lymphoma). This type of blood cancer is known to be aggressive, but often, it will respond to treatment. The oncologist later confided that it was the worst case he had ever seen.

There was hope among doctors that the tumors would respond well to treatment, so they quickly began the "gold standard" of treatments. That was six rounds of the chemotherapy regimen referred to as "R-CHOP" during the spring and summer of 2019. Ruth fared well during treatments, with almost none of the nausea and sickness that many people experience. She did, however, lose hair as predicted and felt increased fatigue.

The treatments were completed in August of that year. The follow-up PET scan showed what doctors called a complete response to treatment. The difference from a few months before seemed miraculous. It appeared that the tumors had, indeed, responded well to treatment. They seemed to be all gone.

We returned home following the final treatment to a banner hung on our garage door by church friends saying, "It's Over!" and flowers delivered to our back porch. It was a collective celebration and sigh of relief with friends across the country who had prayed for and supported us. Now came the slow but much-anticipated recovery period when we hoped strength, stamina, and immunity would return. We knew it would take time, but Ruth made it known she planned to resume teaching duties in a couple of months on November 1, 2019.

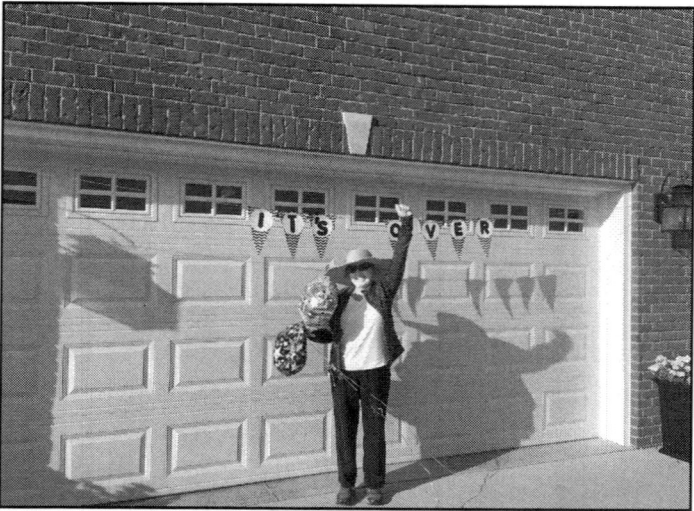

Celebrating what we thought was the last chemo treatment

The recovery began slowly, as expected. We had to move at a slow pace, but gradually, Ruth began to feel stronger. In late September, she felt well enough to take on a task that may have been too much. She decided to wash the dirt and dog tracks off the front porch. Ruth armed herself with a bucket, rags, a broom, and the water hose. She hosed off the porch, got down on her hands and knees, and scrubbed off the dirt. Unsurprisingly, the work made her very tired. Little did we know that this was the beginning of a long, dark journey.

That night or the night after, Ruth began feeling pain in her right elbow and right leg. The pain gradually spread into both of her legs and hands. She had trouble resting and sleeping. She would toss and turn all night. The situation worsened over the next couple of weeks until finally, her legs became so weak that she had a couple of falls.

Ruth was admitted to our local hospital—Owensboro Health Regional Hospital in Owensboro, Kentucky. Many tests followed, including MRIs of different parts of her body. One brain MRI in October holds a lot of irony in our story, which would come to light later. That test showed absolutely no problem or abnormal masses. Meanwhile, no one could determine a cause for her condition. After two weeks of hospitalization, she was transferred to our hospital's rehabilitation wing for more treatment—mainly for physical, occupational, and speech therapy. Speech therapy was recommended because Ruth began having trouble swallowing.

She underwent more tests for possible causes, yet nothing could be determined, and nothing seemed to help. We eventually transferred Ruth to the University of Kentucky Albert B. Chandler Hospital, where she came under the attending care of neurologists. Unfortunately, no solution could be found. They assumed the chemotherapy drug vincristine caused her condition, and that the only way to help her was through intensive therapy and waiting for the passage of time.

Ruth transferred to Cardinal Hill Rehab Hospital in Lexington and spent a few weeks there. Strides of improvement were minuscule in the rehab facility, but there was reason to hope. Unfortunately, the hope I held seemed to be fading in Ruth's mind and in her changing personality. She dearly missed her new home, her dog, and her own bed. I was already losing her—that person, who only months before, was so alive, athletic, positive, competitive, and uplifting to other people. At this point (so soon), she seemed to have lost her will to fight. She was no longer the strong person I had known. Little did we know the most brutal battles we would wage were still ahead.

We came home from the rehab facility on December 12, 2019. I planned to partner with healthcare personnel to assist Ruth in rehabilitation using lessons I had learned from the rehab hospital. We both officially retired from education on January 1, 2020, and our new work began. We started home health therapy. I built some parallel bars in the garage for Ruth to work with as her legs gained strength. That exercise required one person in front, holding on to her gait belt, and another following behind her with a wheelchair. I also obtained a state-of-the-art electronic "active and passive" exercise trainer to help strengthen Ruth's legs. Church friends even built a "standing frame" to assist her in gaining strength to stand. We procured all the durable medical equipment we would need for the bedroom and bath. The problem was that she didn't seem to get any better. She only had one session on the parallel bars, a few on the standing frame, and a few on the active and passive trainer.

At the farm with Sally, October 2019

Physically, Ruth seemed to regress rather than progress. Mentally, she already felt she would not be alive much longer. I fought against that notion and would even scold her when she mentioned it (something I now regret). She seemed to have a sixth sense that things were going downhill—terminally. I thought it was her inability to walk that we were contending with, but somehow, she knew it was more.

Over the next couple of weeks, getting her to eat, think positively, and move around was a struggle. Her lethargy and lack of nourishment led us back to the local emergency room on January 4, 2020. While there, a CT scan showed an abnormal mass in her brain. A brain MRI showed three lesions that did not belong. (The brain MRI just two and a half months before, in October, showed no abnormalities.) A radiologist friend of mine reexamined that report and confirmed there was no sign of any problems. The tumors were fast-growing, and something microscopic must have been at work—too small for the scan to detect in October. The preliminary hypothesis turned out to be the correct one and a most desperate one—the systemic lymphoma had returned, now in the brain. Ruth was transferred back to the UK hospital when a room became available.

Doctors at UK confirmed she now had central nervous system lymphoma. They prescribed a typical treatment plan for this type of cancer—a high dose of methotrexate, a second chemotherapy drug, and a "rescue" drug to reverse the harmful effects of the methotrexate on healthy cells. In between each round of high-dose chemo, Ruth spent a few weeks back in the rehab hospital. Each time, her white blood cell count and platelet count dropped dangerously low as the drugs took effect. Tests showed the treatments were only partially successful. The smallest tumor in the brain seemed to disappear, and the largest mass was shrinking, but the middle-sized tumor was actually growing. We went from a poor prognosis to one that was even worse. At this point, the doctors were unsure what course of action would be best. They discussed it and decided to try a "consolidation" of treatments, utilizing "whole-brain" radiation with oral chemotherapy.

Ruth had already been weary of rehab and of attempts to help her for several weeks. Her will to fight was long gone. She didn't really want any more treatment. Who could blame her? Her mind and body had been through so much pain, fear, loss, uncertainty, and struggle that perhaps it was best to cease the punishment. Adding to what I know about Ruth, friends later told me it was only due to her love for me and the thought of me being left alone that she consented to these last-ditch efforts. I'm now certain of that.

She went through eighteen radiation treatments and took daily oral chemo pills. The consolidated treatment took place only on weekdays. We stayed in a Lexington hotel Monday through Friday and came home on the weekends. In reflection, we should have and could have stayed at home to have these same treatments done locally. Days were so miserable for Ruth that at least seeing her dog, cat, and dream home would have lent a measure of quality to life. Being at home during those treatment weeks might have given her more comfort and peace.

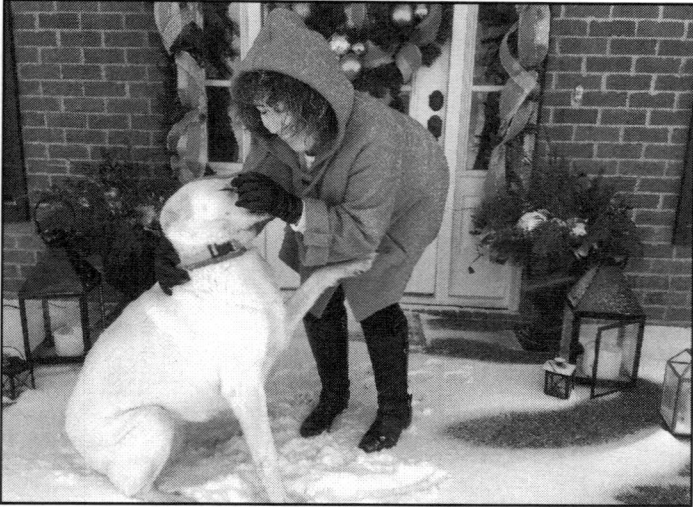

On the front porch with Sally, Christmas 2018

At this point, she had not walked unaided for over four months (since last October), and now she couldn't walk at all. I was hoping and praying that, in some miraculous way, the doctors in this teaching and research hospital would come up with a way to bring Ruth out of the downhill trend she was in. But they were not successful. The end was nearing.

By this time, my wife needed complete, twenty-four-hour care for everything—eating, toileting, bathing, dressing, and mobility. She relied solely on me. Another tragic component of Ruth's story is that, had she been able to walk, she likely would have been a candidate for an autologous stem cell transplant (which involves collecting a patient's healthy blood-forming cells, storing them, and returning them to the patient after treatment). This procedure is very traumatic on one's body, requiring great stamina to survive, but often yields several more years of life for the patient. Because this former tennis player, basketball player, and woman who regularly walked and ran on a treadmill couldn't use her legs at that point, she was denied a chance at what could have been a life-prolonging process.

Following the completion of treatments in Lexington, an MRI of Ruth's brain showed that the tumors were indeed almost completely gone. But her body was spent. Her blood numbers weren't good. The treatments did their job in killing the cancer cells but also deleted her ability to produce healthy new cells. Her body continued to weaken, and her mind seemed to have no fight or positivity. She became even more helpless. Our local oncologist conferred with the UK oncologist and advised us to start hospice care. We enrolled in services, but that time was short. I'm thankful our two boys and their wives were with us to help and love on Ruth during those last days. Several dear friends also came to lend a hand. In a couple of weeks, her battle was over. Then my biggest battle ensued. Ruth was gone.

3

How to Grasp the Grief

Have you ever tried to describe a feeling, moment, or experience so intense that words were inadequate? That's been me so many times, trying to convey in words an ongoing experience that feels indescribable. Yet, trying to describe my loss to friends, colleagues, and counselors felt like a way to cope. Perhaps what I really needed was a way to explain this to myself.

For me, there was numbness for a few weeks. Things that had brought me comfort in the past gave me none. Everything fell short—songs of hope, scripture verses, encouraging cards and letters, uplifting words from friends. None of these provided relief from the mental and emotional pain. We who have loved for an extended time and lost may take some comfort, if only a tiny bit, from knowing that others are experiencing similar struggles. For me, it's hard to describe the struggle adequately, in simple terms, for those who have not experienced this type of loss. It is so multifaceted—much more complex than when I lost each of my parents.

Following are some of my thoughts, observations, and attempts to explain and deal with what happened and how my world has changed since Ruth departed. From what counselors tell me and from what I have read, much of this is common and simply a part of grief. Perhaps you have had similar thoughts or can say, "Yes, I understand!" Some of these relate to the yearlong battle with cancer, and others are in response to the loss that finally came. Here's one example of the sensation of having lost my wife—an excerpt from one of my journals two and a half months after her death. I wrote this long before reading any books and learning that other folks also experience these feelings.

> *On September 6, I was reminded of something I have felt many times. Since she left me, it's as if my life is on "stand still" while others' lives keep on moving. Even my boys have wives and jobs to return to. I have no job, no wife, and worse, with her gone, it seems I have no life. She wasn't just my wife; she was my life. My identity was sewn up into hers, and I can't seem to exist without her. I do exist, but my life has been ripped from me. As I have for weeks, once again, I noticed that I experience pain when my Sunday School class friends are talking about*

their lives, their families, and their activities. No one seems to understand what turmoil I go through just listening to them during our online meetings or in our casual time sitting around the pergola near the lake in our friends' subdivision. Last night, I couldn't stand it. It was painful as they talked about their canoe and white-water trips. I think I concealed it, but I was growing more and more impatient. Why sit and listen? It only reminds me of my times with Ruth and the times I will not get to experience with her. So I've decided I don't want to attend next week. I may just avoid the group until I can feel differently.

And here's another benchmark entry from what I call *My Grief Journal* on December 2, 2020.

This is my NEW NORMAL: to feel a heavy heart most of the time, a veil of darkness over my emotions most of the time, crying most days, if not all, crying multiple times a day on some days while still going through motions to live. Understanding that THIS is the way I will feel, and just going through the motions anyway—eating, shopping when needed, cooking, being with friends, bathing, picking up limbs, mowing, cleaning house. Yearning for more of Ruth Harrison, obsessed with our past and her past, and wanting to connect with her more. Realizing the pain and emptiness of the huge void, realizing it was our relationship and our intimacy that's gone, and praying God will fill that void in his way. I know his time is not my time, but I sure do pray He will fill it.

One month later, I again documented the new normal. It was my son's birthday. Here's part of that day's entry in *My Grief Journal*.

The NEW NORMAL is easy to describe. Heavy sadness upon waking, heavy sadness upon going to bed. Avoiding going to bed. Extreme loneliness. Difficulty dealing with Ruth not being with me (feeling that void sensation over and over). Thinking of Ruth most of the waking hours—our life together, our trips, our homes. The only breaks come when forced to think of something else or when doing something with friends. What's NOT easy to describe is the depth of the sadness, loss, and loneliness.

Sometimes, the new normal is so unpleasant I have "taken off" a few minutes to fantasize. I've imagined what life would be like now if Ruth were with me. I've wondered how we'd have navigated the COVID-19 pandemic together, staying home and doing online work. She had planned to work a few more years during my early retirement, and I've created a pleasant picture in my mind of what that would look like. This January 6, 2021, journal entry describes that vision.

HERE'S MY PLAN FOR LIFE NOW IF SHE WAS WITH ME: I'm retired, taking care of the little farm. Ruth is working, and we've been discussing how or if we can pay off the house this year. She should retire soon, so we are working toward this being her last year of work.

We hole up at home during this COVID-19 mess. I'm teaching Sunday School again, even on Zoom. I help clean the house, and sometimes, she gives me a little job or two to do. She shows me or tells me what she uses or how she does it, and I do it while she's at work.

Sometimes, when she comes home, I have a meal started or prepared. Or we meet at a restaurant somewhere to eat. During COVID, we plan little trips to see friends or family, even if it's a quickie or drive-by. We're planning to go to Alaska together, and maybe back to our favorite little place in Port Isaac, Cornwall, England, or back to Ireland, and to see more of Scotland. I would do some substitute teaching to make a little extra money for trips. We'll pay off the house this year. We sing in the choir and together onstage at church. During COVID, she and I help our music minister on the platform. I lead worship sometimes when he is out of town.

We take trips to the farm in Christian County to walk around with our dog, Sally. We practice target shooting sometimes.

But it's not my plan that counts.

Retirement began a little earlier and quite differently than I had planned. A few months into Ruth's physical struggle, my new job became taking care of my wife. Now, with her gone, I'm trying to come to terms with life anew and answer questions like "Who am I now? Who will I be? What will I do? How will I move forward? What will I enjoy?" (There was a period when I wondered if I would ever enjoy anything again.) I have also wondered how I will manage my mental, emotional, and physical health struggles.

A strange aspect of grief is that things seem more difficult and complex than before—exponentially and indescribably more difficult and complex.

Dualities

These difficulties include what I call "dualities" (or perhaps they are paradoxes) of my grief.

There were things I knew I could do to pass the time, and there were many things that needed to be done around the house and property. I even made a three-page list of things that needed attention. Yet I just didn't have any motivation. I sometimes recorded musings in my daily journal, such as, "It's 7:00 p.m., three hours before I go to bed. What will I do with all that time?"

Closely related to the "lots to do, but no motivation to do it" syndrome, I have sometimes felt anxious or almost excited to do things that cross my mind, even having the motivation to accomplish them. The problem was that I would soon seem to get "paralyzed" mentally, unable to decide on anything.

I have increasingly not wanted to face the friends in my Bible study class, whether live, on Zoom, or at the Sunday night gatherings. Yet I feel intense loneliness and the need to be with someone for companionship, to talk with someone.

I have felt that I could never love and commit to a woman again the way I did with Ruth, yet I sense a profound need to have female companionship and closeness.

Other Complexities

Emotions. Strong and intense, like never before.

Loneliness. Deafening. Excruciating. (The COVID-19 pandemic probably accentuated the loneliness.)

Mental battles. Ongoing and unrelenting.

Tears. Flowing more than ever before and more than I would have ever thought possible.

Longing. Stronger and more pervasive than I've ever experienced before, with a need to express my love for Ruth still, to hold her in my arms and tell her one more time how much I love her, to relive many of our joyous moments together, to express myself to someone, and to share intimate conversations.

Regrets. I know there is little to gain by dwelling on things that could or should have been done. I must admit some of my regrets, however. I don't know if such thoughts are helpful to the grieving process, but they are real and do pass through one's mind. Should I have done this or tried that? Why didn't we go somewhere else for treatment or seek a different opinion? Probably like many others going through grief, I wish I'd realized just how good we had it back when things were "normal." On my part, I sometimes took Ruth for granted and didn't show the appreciation that was due. There's regret for sometimes not being completely honest about my feelings. Now, I see how that would have helped our relationship rise to an even higher level. I even feel regret for "being me," with a personality that works to take care of all the details and cover all the bases (very task-oriented) while sometimes failing to "smell the roses" each day in all things.

To enjoy life and its activities, large and small, was one of my wife's great strengths, but not so much mine. Though I worked as a tireless caregiver and showed my love by being committed to her care, I feel I should have spent more time just being with her and loving on her. Interestingly, each time I had to transfer her from wheelchair to car, bed to chair, chair to couch, or somewhere, I had to pick her up to move her. She called that a "bear hug." It was the same process used by some of the caregivers in the hospitals. Now I look back sadly, realizing that I rarely hugged her during those months to give comfort and affection—just because I loved her. Looking back, I'm sure she would have enjoyed that, and it may have helped her battle the depression and despair that her declining health had brought on.

Then a difficult week in March comes to mind when, due to COVID-19, the rehab hospital prohibited family members from going in and out of the facility. I had a choice to either stay in Ruth's room until she was to be discharged a week later or to depart and not return until that discharge date to pick her up. For various reasons, I decided not to stay. It doesn't matter now that I had a sore throat back then, that I thought I would need all my strength and health to care for her after discharge, or that nights in the facility were noisy and uncomfortable. What seems to matter now is that it was a very difficult time for Ruth, as she couldn't even use a phone without aid and felt distraught and lonely. Her mind was full of despair, and she had to spend almost all of that time alone.

Withdrawal symptoms. My dependency on Ruth developed over time and vice versa. We had a good addiction—each other. Our chemistry was evident in courtship, but a partnership emerged in earnest once we were married. We relied on each other. Having been accustomed to living with a woman for nearly thirty-five years, the days, hours, and minutes without Ruth now are long and lonely. The simple comfort of having someone next to you in bed every night should not be underrated. Sharing about your day and struggles with someone regularly is healthy. Having a trusted advisor with you whenever you need them helps with decision-making. Having a partner who enjoys traveling and playing games with you makes life more fun. Ruth and I shared a love for pets, yard work, and exploring nature, too. Having a musical partner to sing and perform with is quite fulfilling for a musician. Having a member of the opposite sex who takes joy in building you up and who is proud to "belong" to you is the ultimate esteem builder. My intimacy with Ruth existed on physical, emotional, spiritual, and intellectual levels. Now that my spouse is gone, I realize how crucial each aspect of intimacy is. There's the matter of faith that I'll touch on in the next chapter. For now, I'll simply say we held the same beliefs in God and practiced our faith together at home, at church, and as co-leaders in ministry. These connections with my spouse helped to seal our lifelong commitment and kept it going. When all of these things (and more) are gone overnight, how does one describe it? Suffering "withdrawal symptoms" seems inadequate. Going through severe withdrawal comes closer.

Analogies

There are analogies that attempt to explain grief. I'm constantly desiring to tell someone how much this hurts. The pain and the void go so deep that many friends, including counselors, have difficulty understanding the depth of my struggle. So I've often considered ways to explain it to them. I found a few analogies that come close.

New Eyes

The first analogy is simple enough. It's now as if I'm looking at everything in the world through a different set of eyes or a new pair of glasses.

Cut in Half

The second one goes a little deeper and is not so gentle an image. One day, in an attempt to comfort me, a friend struggled to find the right words. He stated, "I know it must be like trying to walk around on one leg now." I quickly explained that it did not seem that way to me at all. Rather, it was more like a huge sharp blade had swung down from above and cut me in half vertically. Half of me was lying on the ground, bloody and lifeless, while the other half was standing there, gazing at the mess, yet frozen in time, unable to act or move.

A Nightmare

The third analogy is for anyone who's had a bad dream, a nightmare, or a dream that evoked intense emotion of some kind. When we wake up from a nightmare, we feel, if only for a few minutes, a lot of emotion. The emotion could be fear, anger, longing, joy, or whatever. In my experience, loss is like retaining the leftover emotion of a bad dream and either not fully coming out of the dream or never relinquishing that heightened level of emotion. This is the sensation that's fueled my turmoil on many occasions—high-octane negative emotion.

A Void That Cannot Be Filled

Then there is the analogy of a void that cannot be filled. Decades ago, on the site where our new house was built, there was an old farmhouse. Just before we began building, there was a mobile home on the site. During our construction process, we discovered a hole in the ground that appeared to be a well or cistern. There was water in the hole. The contractor thought he could simply fill the hole with sand or soil. He dumped a truckful of dirt into the well. To everyone's surprise, the materials simply disappeared. There was apparently more of a void than we realized. The process was repeated with rocks and then more soil. The well was filled eventually. As it relates to my grief, the void I feel in the absence of Ruth seemingly can't be filled. I try to cope in different ways, but this emptiness seems endless, like a cosmic vacuum that can't be satisfied.

A Parallel Universe

Yet another way to explain my experience can be found in literature and science fiction. Authors and movie directors have taken and run with an interesting theory that began in the 1950s. The many-worlds interpretation says that many universes (likely an uncountable number) coexist with our own. Scholars and scientists discuss this theory in relation to cosmology, quantum mechanics, and philosophy. Authors and movie directors exploit it in science fiction books and productions.

Each of the Star Trek franchises created episodes that, due to some accident or ion storm-type phenomenon, found the characters stuck in a parallel world. Stargate SG-1 had Dr. Daniel Jackson walk through a "quantum mirror" into another existence. In the parallel universe, the characters looked much the same, had the same names, and the places and spaceships looked the same. But the characters played different roles. (See Star Trek, season 2, episode 4, "Mirror, Mirror" and Stargate SG-1, season 1, episode 20, "There But for the Grace of God.") A similar example from literature is found in C.S. Lewis's Chronicles of Narnia series, where he creates for the reader two separate but coexisting universes where children from WWII-era England exist elsewhere as kings and queens. In the first book, *The Lion, The Witch, and the Wardrobe*, the children pass through a spare room wardrobe to travel between worlds. The big difference in this story is that the two worlds weren't nearly identical like those in the science fiction examples.

My existence sometimes feels like I've been transported into a strange, different universe. It's almost identical to my own but with fundamental differences. I am in an alternate universe and cannot return to my own familiar one. My new universe does not have Ruth Harrison in it. Everything I do, every place I go, and every relationship I have seems different, yet in other ways, the world is the same as before. My house is the same, but it feels foreign. The change or "transportation" happened the instant she passed from this world, just as it happened for those who were transported onto the "alternate" USS *Enterprise.*

In this new world, I don't have a job (because I had voluntarily retired to take care of Ruth). I was once an engaged educator teaching youngsters music. But for now, I have no desire to return or even to substitute teach. It seems as though that was another person in another life. Though not working, I still have to decide how to spend each day and night. In this universe, I'm very lonely and sad much of the time. Vic Harrison, in the "other" world, was very active in ministry and would gladly sing in public, lead worship, and lead Bible studies. In this world, he has an aversion to speaking or singing in public and is loath to sing in a public church service. He doesn't even want to pray out loud while others listen. He's also not inclined to teach a Bible study group as he did before. This parallel world finds him with low motivation, low confidence, low desire, little sense of purpose, and a lack of identity.

The man in the other universe wanted to travel (with his wife), but this guy has no desire. In the other reality that man sang songs of joy, comfort, and hope in worship services, at weddings, and at funerals to help comfort other people and to connect with God. That fellow also read and quoted Scripture to find rest, hope, and strength. He used Scripture to help other people through their troubles and sorrows. In the new, parallel world, this man knows the songs, and he knows Scripture, but they seemingly do not help him.

That man in the other world thought he knew and practiced faith. He experienced God's peace that was beyond understanding (Philippians 4:7). But this man, in the parallel universe, holds faith in something that he cannot see (Hebrews 11:1) and is waiting for comfort to come. His faith is being tried in this world as it never was before.

The weather is similar in both universes—sun and rain, cloudy or clear, warm and cold, windy or still. The emotional state in the new world is almost always gloomy, stormy, and cold, with very little sunshine. Sometimes, it's just a sad feeling. Sometimes, it's intense longing for the one I lost, and sometimes, it's truly like mental torture. Sometimes, the turmoil and gloom seem constant and unrelenting. The days are bad enough, but nights are the worst. For some unexplained reason, Sunday nights seem to be worse than any other night.

There is also more indecision for me in this universe. So many times, I can't decide what to do. My mind seems to jump from one thing to another, often not completing a thought or a task. There is more mental clutter. So many thoughts and questions and plans are there, all at the same time, but it's hard to organize them or put them away and just "chill." There are times when I simply have a paralysis of the mind. I can't do anything. The only thing I want to do is lie down or sit down, numb. All of these factors definitely make life seem more complicated. This parallel universe is not where I would consciously choose to live. The job, now, is how to navigate through this new parallel universe. The reality that I have to come to grips with is this: I do now live in this universe, and there is no turning back to the old one.

So here I am, feeling the absolute weakest, most distraught, most empty, most lost, most alone, not the least bit confident, and sensing little direction for life. This is the time when I am required to "walk through new, deeper waters," "take steps in the darkness," "go where I have never gone before," and "set sail to an unknown destination." This is what it feels like. I readily admit I need help. And it so happens that someone greater and stronger is available to help.

NOTE: Thanks be to God that much improvement has happened in this area in the last months of this first year!

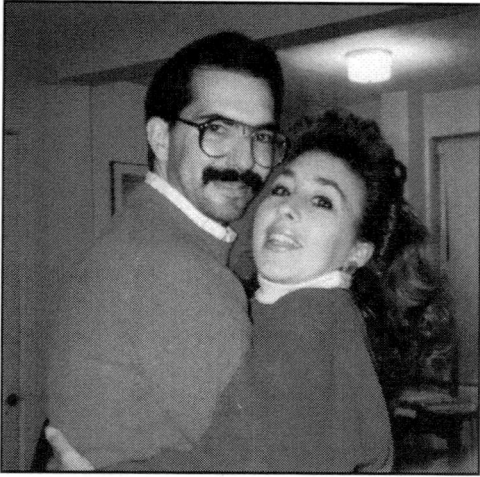

In the Seminary Village apartment, 1987

4

What's Faith Got to Do with It?

So I'm asking the Lord to answer this one prayer:
When he's walking with you in Heaven above,
Would he tell you how I still care?
And that I'm going to be fine,
Though I don't know how.
There's so much that I still can't see.
But I know the One who's holding your hand
Is able to carry me.

From "Without You" by Vic Harrison
February 2021

These are words of confidence—by someone who knows with certainty where his loved one is and that Jesus cares for those left behind. However, I must confess that I wrote these words when I felt uncertain—when my confidence was at an all-time low. This chapter attempts to bridge the gap between what I've believed for many years and what I've felt these last several months. It's a pivotal chapter in that this is where all people can find help from a higher power—the highest power, in fact—our Creator.

Each person's grief journey is unique to them, as is a person's faith journey. Life itself is a journey. Change happens. Even when comfortable in our skin, we're always progressing. From birth to death, our bodies and minds mature as we move from one chapter to another.

Maturity doesn't just happen in the physical and emotional realms, however. The Christian faith is a pilgrimage. And for the believer, it doesn't stop when we die. Here on earth, that journey begins by accepting the gift of God's son, Jesus Christ. Those who believe in Jesus aim to become like Jesus as they grow and mature. Christians achieve that with varying measures of success. We encounter bumps, curves, hills, valleys, trials, and storms on life's journey. Losing my wife is the greatest trial I've experienced by far. But God's Word tells me trials develop my faith and mature me (James 1:2–4).

The best is yet to come—life with our Lord in Heaven in the afterlife. Ruth is there now. I've been taught this since childhood, and I've affirmed this as an adult. I've found the passages, read, studied, and believed them. I've been in a position to teach others how the Bible speaks to these truths. I've sung songs and shared Bible verses through the years to encourage those who were struggling with the illness and death of loved ones. Ruth knew and loved these same songs and verses. She and I shared the same belief in Jesus. We openly practiced our Christian faith at home with family and at work with colleagues. That's one reason we had a good marriage.

Some spiritual words in this chapter may be hard to understand or accept for those unfamiliar with this faith (1 Corinthians 2:14). Ruth and I unashamedly used our faith to direct our daily lives and decisions. I cannot help but lean on the Christian faith now to work through this grief. If I don't, then my words, songs, and teaching from the past would all be a lie.

But just because my faith in Christ is sincere does not mean my grief is easy to deal with. We are not given a pass from terrible heartache because we have and exhibit faith. We are still human beings, gifted by God with emotions and needs. We can't expect God to take them away amid loss. For me, they are front and center. Faith enables me to hang on even when the way isn't clear. And when I don't get what I want. Through Ruth's illness, it was my prayer and the prayer of many others across the country that Ruth would come through the illness and continue to live and enjoy life here on earth. That was the type of healing we were asking for. But I've learned through the years that while prayers seem to go unanswered, those requests are answered, albeit in a way I did not intend. Ruth has experienced total healing now, but not in the way we desired. I wanted to spend more quality time with her here on earth. We had planned to grow old together.

God doesn't always take our difficult struggles away. He certainly has the power to do that, yet he often does not for reasons unknown to us. He does promise to walk with us through dark times—even to carry us. There were dark times in my grief when none of the familiar inspirational songs or Bible verses helped. At first, even that sense of the presence of God was gone. A look at three scenes from my life will help illustrate how different losses have tested my faith. I'm still on this lonely road, but thank God for bringing me far from where I was. Again, this is only my experience.

Losing My Mother

One night in July 2005, I walked out under the stars at my parents' home in Christian County, Kentucky. I had just spent the last eight days watching my mother slowly waste away. Alzheimer's disease had its grip on her. She had stopped eating and drinking and could no longer speak. It wasn't clear how much she knew. Her sweet eyes and smile held me close as I showed her pictures and talked with her day by day. It seemed like she was enjoying our time together, though she couldn't verbalize it. She ended her battle with Alzheimer's that night and entered eternity with Jesus.

A vast void swept in. The woman who raised me, held me, soothed the fever from my brow, taught me, and loved me was gone. I stepped out under the stars in the clear night sky and thanked God for my mother, giving my pain and loss to him. I told him how much I loved her. I would depend on him to help me now. As I looked at the face of God the best I could, he gave me a strange and wonderful peace, even though I was experiencing the worst pain I had ever felt. I claimed the promise in Philippians 4:6–7.

Do not be anxious about anything, but in every situation, by prayer and petition, with thanksgiving, present your requests to God. And the peace of God, which transcends all understanding, will guard your hearts and your minds in Christ Jesus.
Philippians 4:6–7

Losing My Father

Ten years later, in June 2015, I again walked out under the stars at my parents' home. I needed to talk to God. Earlier that morning, I read my dad a Psalm, as I had for the last few days there in the hospital. But this time, he was asleep. After I finished reading and praying, his breathing became labored. It slowed until there was a long pause between each breath. Then . . . he exhaled his last breath on earth.

I drove back to Fearsville that day, where his house was, and bought a bologna sandwich in his honor. He often ate a bologna sandwich for lunch. That night at his house, the sky was clear, and the stars were bright. I walked out and looked up, again imagining I was looking at the face of God. I thanked God for my dad and the joy of caring for him these last few years and for the upbringing, example, and teaching my dad had given me. I asked the Lord to help me. Though I had now lost both of my parents, and my heart was so heavy, I received a peace that I couldn't fully understand. That peace helped me be at ease, even though I felt so empty during this loss.

Losing My Wife

Five years after that, in June 2020, I walked out under the stars at home in Daviess County, Kentucky. I'm unsure how many days it had been, but this was the first clear night since Ruth had gone to live with Jesus. The stars were shining brightly. I looked up at them toward the face of God. I needed to talk to him. I told the Lord how much I loved Ruth and missed her. I thanked God for all the blessings he brought to me through her. Like the stars in the sky that night, there were too many to count. I told him I knew he was there, that he created Ruth and me, and that he brought us together. He was responsible for this blessing. And now she was with him. I asked for his help. But there, under the stars in the presence of God, peace did not come.

I knew God heard my prayer, but I did not feel his presence. I felt alone. I felt empty. I felt unknown. I felt unsure. My heart was more than broken. My heart was torn away.

The juxtaposition was real. I knew and believed that God was in control. He had welcomed my wife to a new life with him that was better than anything here on earth. I trusted he still loved me and cared about my situation. Yet, my heart felt something different. Emptiness, loneliness, and a distinct lack of peace swirled inside me like I had never felt before. I know God gives help to the helpless and hope to the hopeless, but I had never been this helpless or hopeless myself. This was a new experience. Where was my faith?

My faith was there but did not make me immune to suffering. It didn't prevent the loss of my mate long before it should have happened. My faith did not keep me from feeling the pain, denial, and anger that comes with losing one's other half. Faith didn't keep me from wondering why and saying, "This cannot be happening" and "This should not have happened."

As months have passed, I've realized that everything, even this, was an unusual test of my faith. It seems cruel and unusual, but it's not unlike the testing of those heroes of faith we find in Scripture. It's as if the Lord said, "Okay. How will you react to this terrible situation? Will you draw closer to me, rely on me, learn more about me, or turn the other way? Show me what you are made of. Show me how you will use this newfound freedom. I will walk with you."

I'm realizing it takes more spiritual maturity than I had before. Of course, I'd rather not grow this way, but I know now that my faith is growing. It took a few months to finally arrive at a question that was somewhat comforting regarding my faith. "If God has blessed me many times throughout my life (and he has), why would I expect him to stop blessing me now that Ruth is gone?" The answer is obvious—he's not finished blessing me. Even with his blessings, however, my struggle with the pain was and is crushing, as I described in my prayer to him just over two months after Ruth's death.

September 1, 2020

I know I have to experience this. It's so hard and hurts so bad; it's almost unbearable. It makes me crazy. All this heightened emotion all the time and no positive emotions. I have an overwhelming appreciation for what Ruth was and is and how you, Lord, blessed me through her. With all of her greatness, gifted as no other woman I've ever met or known about, you gave her to me; and she gave herself to me. Now, to have lost it feels like it is killing me every day. So . . . I need help. They say I'm doing well, but I'm feeling so lost and undone, bleeding and dying. I'm struggling to feel your presence, grace, and peace. So I'll tell you again—I know you are my rock and my fortress, but I feel so alone. I believe You are doing something, you are working, and you love me; but it's hard to sense. So, Lord, "I do believe, but help me overcome my unbelief!" What do you have in mind for me? Help me to be patient and listen to you. Help me not to rush into anything. Help me not to push. But what do you have in mind?

I documented a similar perspective in my journal just over four months after Ruth's passing. I was reading Isaiah chapter 43 and was especially moved by verses 18–19. My faith grew a little bit as I reasoned through my thoughts.

Forget the former things; do not dwell on the past.
See, I am doing a new thing! Now it springs up;
do you not perceive it? I am making a way in the
wilderness and streams in the wasteland.
Isaiah 43:18–19

October 29, 2020

I DON'T KNOW what this new way is. I don't know how He knit me together (Psalm 139). I don't know how He created this world. I don't know how He arranged for me to meet, date, fall in love with Ruth, have things, do things, go all the places we did, and belong to each other so deeply. I don't know ANY of these. So how could I expect to know what this new way will be? I only know that I have enjoyed what He's blessed me with. What a great life we shared.

The following entry, recorded about two months later, illustrates another step in working out my faith.

January 2, 2021

Something has kept me eating well. Something has made me drive myself to keep exercising, even if it's just walking. I make myself do it even when I don't want to. Though I haven't been feeling the peace of God or His presence like I used to, could it be that these basic things are ways God's grace is keeping me afloat or keeping me going? Some people can't even do these things during grief. I'm sure that the remarkable grace of God brought Ruth and me together. Could it be He's keeping me alive and well with these things I take for granted?

Now, I see that my faith provides me with an entire world of assistance, hope, and support. I didn't realize this as much until the months wore on, but one by one, I could see how God was answering prayers and coming to my aid. Though I may have felt quite alone at times, I have always known God provides for me. Here's how.

My Family
I am blessed to have the support of the family God gave me. Ruth and I were blessed by our two boys and their wives, along with the support of extended family like aunts and uncles and cousins.

My Church Family
Speaking of family, the family of God (our church members) continues to reach out to care for me in my loss in real and precious ways. It's not only my current church family, but also friends from past churches we have been a part of. Sometimes, they are like angels that reach out to comfort me.

Old Friends
I continue to be blessed by people I knew long ago but had lost touch with for one reason or another. Reconnecting with them has brought a degree of enjoyment back into life. Some even offered companionship, which I needed badly.

The Gift of Music

Musical appreciation and skill is a gift from God and has become a source of joy and fulfillment during this loss. I'll explain more fully in the next chapter what part music has played. For now, I'll touch on the spiritual help from hymns. As a worship leader, I have enjoyed the guidance and biblical truth found in the lyrics of many of our Christian hymns. People who've had severe tests and tragedies in life often penned the lyrics, many of which are very appropriate for the grief we encounter. The experiences of believers through the ages have thus aided me in my present grief. I have sung many of these hymns from childhood. And now, as an adult, I see their value to the Christian. It wasn't until I dealt with my current crisis of faith, that I could relate to many of these hymns in my grief. Suddenly, they were about my experience.

Here's a sampling of some hymn lyrics that truly address my experience.

My hope is built on nothing less
Than Jesus' blood and righteousness.

When darkness seems to hide His face,
I rest on His unchanging grace.

WHAT'S FAITH GOT TO DO WITH IT?

When all around my soul gives way,
He then is all my hope and stay.[1]

Have faith in God when your pathway is lonely,
He sees and knows all the way you have trod.

Never alone are the least of His children;
Have faith in God, have faith in God.

Have faith in God in your pain and your sorrow,
His heart is touched with your grief and despair.
Cast all your cares and your burdens upon Him,
And leave them there, oh, leave them there.[2]

While life's dark maze I tread,
And griefs around me spread,
Be thou my guide;
Bid darkness turn to day,
Wipe sorrow's tears away,
Nor let me ever stray
From Thee aside.[3]

1. Edward Mote, "Solid Rock," v 1, v 2, v 3, (1834).
2. B. B. McKinney, "Have Faith in God," v 1, v 2, v 3, (1934).
3. Ray Palmer, "My Faith Looks Up to Thee," v 3, (1830).

The Holy Spirit

Faith teaches us that the Holy Spirit is at work even when we do not realize what he is doing. Often, it is only in hindsight that we understand how God was working in our lives. Faith teaches that we do not have the capacity or understanding to see what beautiful tapestry God may be weaving, even during trials (Romans 8:26–28, James 1:2–4).

His Spirit is at work within us to carry to completion what he started in us (Philippians 1:6). Even though the life I knew seems to have ended, I know his work in me won't end because my partner is gone. I just do not have the answers as to how God will work in me, when it might happen, in what way, or who else will be involved. But his Spirit is alive.

Great Examples from Scripture

My steps into this great unknown world are nothing new to humankind. Not only are many others around me going through similar struggles, but we see examples from biblical history of people who have dealt with difficulties yet moved on due to their strong faith in God. They didn't have the answers or reasons either. But they had faith.

Abraham pulled out all the stops with family and goods and left his home and relatives because God said, "Go." The instructions were to start moving "to a place I will tell you." At first, that was it.

In the book of Judges, Gideon was the youngest of his clan. He lacked confidence and courage but was called a "mighty warrior" by God's angel. The angel told Gideon to "go in the strength you have and save Israel" from the Midianites who were oppressing them. Gideon became a great leader and helped save God's people from a huge army of Midianites and others. Gideon didn't know how God would accomplish it, but God did (Judges 6–7).

In the Old Testament book of Job, we read in-depth about a person who loved God, was dealt unbelievable suffering, yet refused to turn his back on his Maker. Worthy of note for me and for all of us going through grief is that Job was not happy with his situation. He was honest and questioned God, but he never turned against God or cursed him as his so-called friends advised.

The Greatest Example

The greatest example of someone going through indescribable agony is that of Jesus Christ himself. He is the Creator of the universe with the power to speak worlds into existence, yet he willingly confined Himself to a human body and subjected himself to the humility and torture of the crucifixion (Philippians 2:5–8). That's beyond any hardship I have endured.

Though my pain feels like too much to live with at times, it cannot possibly compare with what the Lord experienced. It was his love that empowered him to do that for me and for everyone who receives this gift. This act shows how much the Creator cares for me. Mark Vroegop says in *Dark Clouds, Deep Mercy* (2019, 37), "The cross shows us that God has already proven himself to be for us and not against us."

Isaiah 53:3 is part of a prophecy that foretold how Jesus would become a "man of sorrows and familiar with suffering." Because he did this, I know that God is ready and able to help me.

The Solid Rock

"My hope is built on nothing less than Jesus' blood and righteousness." Even during this time in my life when things don't seem right, one thing is clear—I have a constant. Despite everything else changing in my daily life, one thing remains the same—God, as experienced through Jesus Christ. He is the same yesterday, today, and forever (Hebrews 13:8). I sometimes can't seem to grasp hold of anything in life, but his grace and mercy holds me.

I haven't forgotten the great paradox that, though Christ's love and mercy has never changed, it is new every day (Lamentations 3:22–25). I need that. Without a doubt, one of the most difficult aspects of this grief journey has been to trust in his grace and mercy even when I don't feel his presence or his peace. To be sure, I have cried out to God on many occasions for relief. Even during those times of no relief, I find in his Word a kindred spirit who cried out long before me. Though it was for different reasons, "the one after God's own heart," the future King David shared a terrible sentiment in Psalm 13:1–2 when he said, "How long, Lord? Will you forget me forever? How long will you hide your face from me? How long must I wrestle with my thoughts and day after day have sorrow in my heart?"

During the first few months, it was definitely a struggle to work out my faith and allow God to work. But I never turned my anger toward God the way some do. I'm beginning to understand what faith requires. Interestingly, I've been a believer for over fifty years but am now plunging deeper into what faith really means.

I'm realizing that my relationship with God really is bigger than my relationship with Ruth. I've known that for a long time, but now it's obvious. I don't think I've walked with God like this until now. My relationship with God is more important than my relationship with Ruth. That's hard to say, but it's true. Now she's gone, and I'm still here. But God is with me, and I imagine he expects our relationship to grow now that it's just me and him.

I've also discovered a small, unexpected pleasure—a sense of fulfillment in the midst of all the heartache and struggle. Ruth is now in perfect health with the One who created her. She's experiencing the reward of her faith. This faith began in childhood when she accepted Jesus as her Lord many years ago. Believers in Jesus call this eternal life, but the Bible teaches that eternal life begins when we first accept him. We don't have to wait for that "pie in the sky, by and by, when we die."[4] Part of the gift of eternal life is living a full and meaningful life along the way (John 10:10). Ruth capitalized on living a full and meaningful life more than anyone I've ever known. She influenced me as well as those around her to do so too. My unexpected pleasure is looking into Scripture like never before to help me deal with and process the wake of loneliness following Ruth's death.

God's general plan for each person and each marriage is in the Bible. His plan for my marriage was there too. I look at Scripture now and see my life and Ruth's life in the Word of God. Or perhaps it's more accurate to say I can look back and see God's Word in our relationship. This truth may be hard to convey to those who haven't experienced this type of loss or who don't have this faith. God's grace allowed us to carry out God's original plan for marriage. His plan is always the best way. Even with all our faults and imperfections, I can say we did it his way, as it's spelled out in Genesis and taught by Jesus.[5]

---

4. Joe Hill, "The Preacher and the Slave," (1911).
5. Genesis 1:27, 2:24

*"Haven't you read," he replied, "that at the
beginning the Creator 'made them male and
female,' and said, 'For this reason a man will leave
his father and mother and be united to his wife,
and the two will become one flesh'? So they are no
longer two, but one flesh. Therefore what God has
joined together, let no one separate."*
Matthew 19:4–6

Ironically, after Ruth's death, I'm coming closer to understanding what "one flesh" means. The pain of our separation signifies just how united we were. Yes, we were one physically, but our connection was emotional, mental, and spiritual as well. We were also fruitful and multiplied (Genesis 1:28).

Fortunately, I truly enjoyed "the wife of my youth" (Proverbs 5:18) for many years, unlike some whose marriages end early due to divorce. In my helping Ruth during her illness, my love was patient and kind. It always protected, hoped, and persevered (1 Corinthians 13). Though I felt angry for a while, how could I direct my anger toward God when he's the one who blessed me with Ruth? He's the one who gives me good things. "You are my Lord; apart from you I have no good thing" (Psalm 16:2). That's how I feel and what I tell him! Only after months, though, and with reminders from the likes of Oswald Chambers. In *My*

Utmost for His Highest (January 26), Oswald reminds me we must grow where we are planted, just as the "lilies of the field" (Matthew 6:28–29). I am now "planted" in a new situation.

There's a phrase Ruth and I used to say to express gratitude: "Praise God, it's his fault!" Ruth kept every card and letter I ever sent her—from our dating months through our marriage years. After losing her, I read through them to hold on to her. On one of the cards I sent to her during our courtship was that phrase I started saying years ago. I discovered she had kept some cards that she sent me, also. She'd written that phrase to me on a card as well. A dear member from one of our churches who used to video our events presented me with three DVDs that included songs and programs Ruth and I had performed. One of them was a video of our "farewell" service at that church. On the recording, I thanked the church for ministering alongside Ruth and me. I concluded my address to the church by telling them to "Praise God, it's his fault!"

When I look back on my life with Ruth, I can see God with us throughout our story. He brought us together and gave us the years we shared, so I am very blessed. My struggle isn't over, but my faith is growing. My faith is being tested, but God is good. "It's his fault!" I'm thankful Ruth preserved the very first card where I coined that phrase. It was a Christmas card I sent to her in 1984, about one month prior to our engagement.

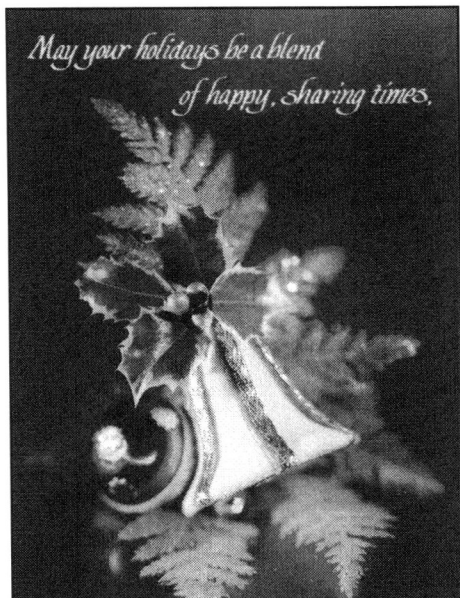

May your holidays be a blend
of happy, sharing times,

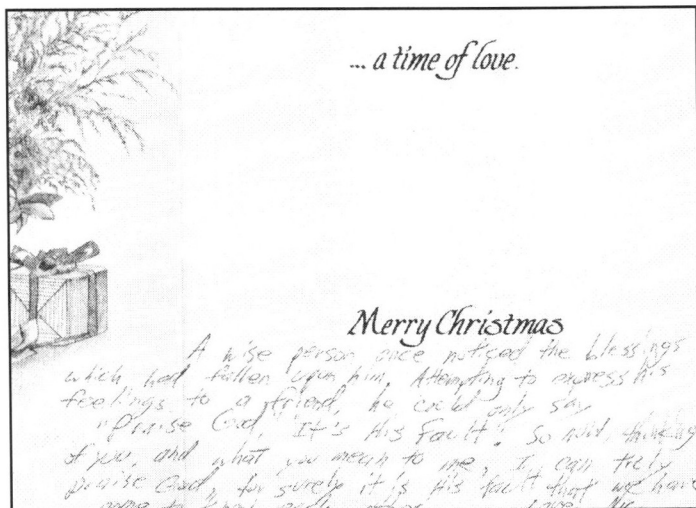

... a time of love.

Merry Christmas

A wise person once noticed the blessings
which had fallen upon him. Attempting to express his
feelings to a friend, he could only say
"Praise God, It's His Fault!" So now, thinking
of you, and what you mean to me, I can truly
praise God, for surely it is His fault that we have
come to know each other ...

"Praise God, it's his fault!"

63

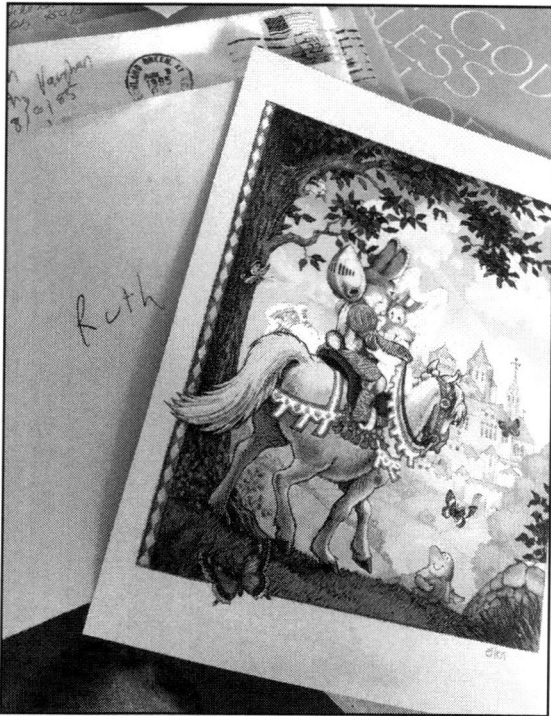

"Would you mind terribly if I loved you for a lifetime?"
Just before our wedding, July 1985

5

Where to Go from Here

Where to go from here? How to live this life?
How to face each day without my love, my wife?
Oh, the questions now are many,
But the answers are so few.
And the biggest question for me now is,
How to live without you?

From "Without You" by Vic Harrison
February 2021

The first anniversary of my wife's passing is approaching. This has been a terrible year of "firsts." Each one has challenges of its own—the first marriage anniversary without her, the Thanksgiving holiday, her birthday, my birthday, Christmas, New Year's, and Valentine's Day. Even the 20th of each month has been gloomy and dark (the day she passed away). As the last first approaches, I'm nowhere close to feeling settled or satisfied in my new life. As my faith grows, however, and as time passes, I have gained a new perspective. I look back and can see that I've made progress.

This chapter will list specific steps I've taken. I don't address every practical matter, like what to do with a loved one's clothes, shoes, and belongings. (Although, that's important and can be a source of stress for many surviving spouses.) I'm here to address the emotional, mental, and philosophical questions that have come to mind.

What happens now that life has drastically changed, and I no longer have a partner to share it with? How do I proceed? How does anyone proceed? What will I feel like in two years? In five years? Will I ever have a loving relationship again? Will I remarry? Will I ever travel again to the places we visited and wanted to return to? Will I travel by myself? What will I do with my time? My money? How will I manage the house and property by myself? Will I ever return to teach in the Bible study class where Ruth and I shared the leadership? Will I reconnect with people Ruth and I used to socialize with? What about those relationships in which Ruth was the driving force in bringing us together? Will I maintain them? What work does God have for me in his plan?

In this healing process, where daily tasks have become difficult, moving on with life is just as hard. Every person's situation is different, but perhaps my experiences will resonate with someone. Maybe some of my actions will help stir ideas for others.

I didn't feel like I was progressing for the first few months. I didn't know what progress was, but I certainly didn't think I was making any. I even prayed, "Lord, how long will I be stuck in this deep sadness? When will I begin to dig out of this hole? When will I feel like I'm getting better? Please let me know when I am making progress." That is just one of several laments I made to the Lord. Life was hard, so I started reaching out in several directions. The good news is that the Lord did begin to answer prayers. Here's what I started doing.

Reaching Out to Other Widowers and Widows

My efforts to reach out for help included speaking with other widowers and widows about their situations. In my current church family, there is no shortage of those who have lost their spouses in the last few years. Interestingly, these less-than-inspirational quotes came from conversations with them:

"You'll find your new normal someday. After nearly two years, I haven't found mine yet."

"I have a new life now. I don't like my new life."

"Let me warn you, it doesn't get any better."

"It took me two years before I had any peace."

Within these negative sentiments, I found one positive aspect. They told me I was not alone in what I was experiencing. Someone else understood the depths of my experience. These people could readily sympathize and empathize with me because they had been there too. Because I desired to share the company of someone else who had lost their spouse, because we have so many of those people in our church, because there is such a great need, and as a way of connecting with Ruth, I began to occasionally host a lunch for a small group of widows and widowers. I sent invitations asking them to attend my "Club of Hearts." Ruth was such a great hostess that I felt connected with her when I cooked for and hosted others.

It just so happens that two of my guests who came to the first group lunch had a meeting outside afterward. She asked him if he would like to go out for coffee sometime. They began dating and, as of this writing, are newlyweds! They had not been looking for someone to remarry but to share companionship with. One thing led to another, and now, in their seventies, they plan to spend the rest of their lives together.

Journaling

To be sure, for months I felt a thick covering of gloom and sadness all around me. After a few months of constantly clouded sky, there were only a few minutes, on two different days, where I did feel a little hope—a brief ray of sunshine, if you will. That's not much daylight! I can pinpoint those times and dates, reflect on them, and see progress because I journaled about them.

I share them now because it's significant that at least there was some measure of hope, even if very short-lived and only for two days. With God answering prayer and with time, those brief moments of sunshine have slowly increased. Now, there is an equal amount of sun and cloudiness. I even had a couple of months when things felt so good, there was more sunshine than cloudiness. For me, that happened at about the eight-month mark. Journaling is a concrete, practical, and valuable practice that can help someone understand what they are going through.

During Ruth's illness, I began keeping a log of some things. For one, I wanted to keep up with her needs and document when things didn't go well at a facility, whether the hospital or the rehab hospital. To be a patient advocate for my wife, I needed good documentation. At home, I wanted to keep up with her vital signs, the physical therapy I could help with, and her food and fluid intake to share the information with medical professionals. These logs became where I could also record my feelings and struggles. They were where I voiced prayers, concerns, and complaints to God. Some of them were laments as I cried out to him for help.

After her death, I continued journaling daily events, thoughts, and laments. My daily log contains several details from each day. In a second document, I record highlights of my grief journey chronologically. I call this document *My Grief Journey*, and it starts about two and a half months after Ruth's passing. This is the journal I look at to see the benchmarks or milestones of my progress.

My counselor encouraged me to continue these logs. I began using them intentionally to chart my journey and for perspective on my progress. Looking back on these journals helps me gauge where I have been and where I am now. Not to mention, it helps me to see how God has answered prayer. Five months into the process, on November 25, after spending time reading through my journals, I added this milestone to *My Grief Journey* document:

> *I think I'm discovering that what I'm doing is gradually reconstructing my life. It's a slow process, but I've been taking steps to help me move through this journey, even with the seemingly slow pace.*

I am reconstructing life. That's one way I sometimes look at my situation, for it seems the life I had has crumbled.

That is how it often feels—actual, imagined, or somewhere in between. Perhaps it is not a drastic rearrangement for others, but for me, it is. Journaling helps me see the direction of my steps and how I'm piecing life together again.

I want to reiterate that there is no standard timetable during which one should experience certain things. Time and progress may move slowly. Whether it takes a few months, many months, years, or however long, when someone is ready, they will do the thing. In other words, one will take steps to move on through life in one's own time. No one can point to a certain date and say, "By this point in time, you should have done this and that." The caution here is not to become frozen in time so you never take a step forward.

Professional Counseling

For years, I have kept in touch with a former pastor, Dr. Melvin Felts, who is now a certified biblical counselor. What a blessing! It's often helpful to talk one-on-one with someone trained in counseling. They can see the big picture objectively and give helpful suggestions. Professional advice is invaluable when navigating uncharted waters. Though Dr. Felts is about eighty miles away, I see him every few weeks to touch base, share, and seek input.

Dr. Felts gave me many great pieces of advice (and still does). One of them was to revisit my journal entries—not just write one and never return to it. A repetitive look at those entries could help me see how God works through my experiences and interactions with others. He was correct! It's been very helpful to periodically go back and reread what I've recorded.

Another suggestion was "Don't get stuck where you are." He said that some people, even those who take the positive step of going for counseling, want to relive the grief and keep reliving it. Everyone needs time to dwell on grief, but he said some folks tend to stay in it.

He also advised me to busy myself in some projects, but not to get too busy. Well-meaning friends may tell you to stay busy, and I've experienced that. Especially since I'm retired, some have said, "You need to get another job." Staying busy can be a way to keep from wallowing in grief. But my counselor also warns against people being so busy, and perhaps getting busy too soon, that they fail to continue to seek ways to deal with their grief. Busyness can be good or it can be a way to avoid healthy grieving. This grief journey is not an enjoyable ride. Still, my sage counselor advised me to look for things I can experience on this journey. He asked, "What is it that God has around you that you might miss out on by being too busy?"

I have sought to keep my eyes open. As I deal with my grief, it's good to be reminded to keep looking for what God has in store. Granted, at first, I was not ready for that advice. I was just struggling to breathe and survive. But the passage of time does allow for a change in perspective, to a degree. When a person is ready and able to, I highly recommend seeking a biblical counselor for solid assistance.

Reading Books about Grief

I could hardly bear to read anything the first couple months after Ruth passed. When I felt ready, I was glad to receive books from my counselor and several friends. I even searched online and found a couple of other helpful websites and books. Some books have been well-suited for my situation, and others are more about grief in general. Though none of them were filled with words just for me, all of them had some insights and descriptions that were very helpful. They reminded me I'm not the only one going through this type of tragedy. And they helped me identify and better name some of the issues I could relate to.

For example, one book I read three months in identified the different types of intimacy I was missing. It helped affirm that emotional loneliness, a lack of someone to share with, and not having an intimate confidante are common, deep-seated needs. Through reading, I've been able to take a more objective look at what my needs may be and how to approach relationships going forward.

Getting Through Each Moment with Variety

I sometimes had to give myself some advice just to get through a day. The poem "A Grandmother's Advice" by Elena Mikhalkova is a good perspective on moving forward slowly. Here's a note to myself:

As you try to get through one day at a time, even one hour at a time, even a few minutes at a time, give yourself some breaks—do various things. Spend a little time on one thing, then another thing. Allow variety because you can get so burned out and so depressed by staying on one thing. For you, it's reading, playing hymns, writing music, just doodling on the piano, reading the newspaper, walking the farm, weed trimming, walking/riding/jogging the Greenbelt, surfing the internet, writing, cooking, taking food to people, etc.

Eating

One of my widowed friends told me she had difficulty eating well after her husband passed. That is one thing I've remained consistent with. I have realized that when very little brings me joy, I receive some measure of joy from simply preparing and eating good meals. I am very thankful for that.

Exercising

Even during the first few months when life was very gloomy, I regularly walked or rode my bike. I even went further than usual. I'll admit that the extra steps were just to avoid sitting or staying in one place all the time. I was so distraught that I needed to go somewhere and do something. I intentionally chose to get up and walk or ride a bike instead of doing detrimental things to my body. I walked or rode my bike aimlessly just to kill time and get from one hour to the next. I was desperate to pass time because much of it was hard to endure. I knew that walking or riding for extended periods of time would be doing my body a favor. I hoped it would help my mental well-being also. I think it did. Going to the paved path in our city known as the Greenbelt was a way for me to see other people. Though I often felt like hiding in a corner at home, it was healthy to see other humans each day and say hi, even if I didn't know them. I've even begun running again, something I haven't done in a few years.

Reading and Studying Scripture

Like eating well and exercising, I've made it a priority to read God's Word. The Bible has been special to me most of my life. It's helped guide me in the past, and after Ruth died, I knew I would turn to it again. It took a few weeks, but I did indeed return to it.

The book of Psalms was most helpful. I read through Psalms a few times this first year. Sometimes, I would start at the beginning and sometimes at Psalm 150, reading the chapters in reverse order. King David and other psalmists expressed some of the same feelings I've had. Some of those verses make excellent prayers when we can't adequately voice our feelings. I've claimed their sentiments toward God as my own.

I can't overemphasize the value of extended exposure to God's Word and how helpful it can be. Scripture has played a huge role in the growth of my faith through this grief. It's also been helpful to memorize certain verses so they are always with me.

Celebrating and Sharing

As my soul tried to deal with the loss of my wonderful mate, I felt the need to tell the world about my wife. I needed to proclaim in some way, "Look at what I lost! Look at what I had! Look at what we had! Look at how special Ruth was!" I wanted to celebrate her by telling others about her. After one month had passed, I decided to use social media to share pictures of Ruth and a story each morning in August. I called it "A Tribute to My Wife." Although our anniversary was on August 3, I wanted to take the whole month to share different aspects of my wife. Ruth was so gifted in so many areas and enjoyed so many different things, the job wasn't that hard. The most difficult thing was finding and organizing the photos to use.

Part of celebrating Ruth was walking through the house, finding photos, and organizing them all. This process took time but yielded many old photos I used in my daily posts in August. That laborious process was a way to look back and remember our early years, our dating life, and our adventures together. It was also me hanging on to her. Whether that was healthy or not, I don't know. But at least it was a constructive way to keep busy. And now our photos are better organized, making it easier for our children (and someday grandchildren) to view and enjoy. I like to arrange things logically—to establish a sense of order. Organizing our family photos was a way to do that when my life felt very out of order.

Ruth with our puppy, Victoria

Another way I celebrated my marriage was by watching old videos of our home activities, our church programs, and our solos and duets. Some of these were the videos that friends from former churches gave me after Ruth passed, and some were home videos I recorded when our boys were small. We had all the VHS tapes converted to DVD. However, I can't watch the videos for long periods because it tends to put me in a gloomy mood. I view them in moderation so a celebration doesn't turn into depression.

Playing a diva in a musical at Burlington Baptist

Ruth enjoyed many, many things, to include eating certain foods. She liked Big Mac and Chick-fil-A sandwiches, and she loved ice cream. To celebrate her and connect with her, I will occasionally partake of those foods and fondly remember her. I did that several times with my sons when they were both with me. Their mom also dearly loved Diet Coke before she got sick, and though I am not a fan of diet drinks, I had one to celebrate her. On her 59th birthday, in her absence, I spent the entire day celebrating with foods Ruth had fun with. I took donuts and a picture of Ruth and me to my school and did the same for the staff at the school where Ruth taught. For breakfast I had a sausage McMuffin, for lunch a Chick-fil-A sandwich, and that afternoon, I baked chocolate chip cookies and made chili. Then I hosted a hot dog cookout with some of our best friends (something Ruth loved to do)!

Church Attendance

One week after my wife's funeral, I returned to the worship service at my church. I wasn't feeling particularly spiritual or worshipful. At the time, I'm afraid I had more of a selfish motivation. I went because I was grasping for anything that might give me some relief from the awful mental and emotional pain I was experiencing. Whatever the motivation, is there a better place or better people to hang out with than with Christian brothers and sisters? I knew that hearing hymns, Scripture, prayer, and the sermon in a united worship service had inspired me many times before. I hoped that something I heard might indeed help. (After all, that was why I became a worship leader—to inspire and help others.) It certainly couldn't hurt!

Interestingly, after being a singer and musician for most of my life, I could not sing hymns in church for several months. Whatever I needed to make me sing was not there.

After some of my emotional numbness wore off, however, I began to intently listen to the lyrics and pray them as others sang. Finally, around seven months, I began to sing in church again. By eight months, my heart had enough joy to sing with gusto! I'm thankful God restored that gift.

I've returned to some of my former activities at church, but not all of them yet. I've not resumed my duties as a Bible study teacher during this first year. I have only filled in a couple of times. Ruth was very much a part of the class that we led together. So much so that I have not come to terms with how I will do that. The friends in our Bible study class have been so kind and have reached out in many ways. They would get together at my beck and call and do anything for me, but I'm not comfortable returning to the group yet. I feel like I'll serve again in some capacity, but exactly how, when, and where remains to be seen. The Lord is not finished with me yet, I am certain.

Hanging with Close Friends

There were some couples from our church family and Bible study that Ruth and I socialized with regularly. We met at least one other couple for dinner almost every Friday night. I continue to get together with them regularly to share a meal. I've also begun to cook and invite those couples to my house for meals. I've had up to four couples here at one time for a few fish fries or pancake breakfasts at night. It feels like I'm connecting with my spouse as I host these friends because that's something she excelled at.

Other couples from towns we lived in years ago have kept in touch, and quality time with them is always beneficial. These friends all help fill some of the need for companionship. Some even help with the emotional loneliness that accompanies my grief.

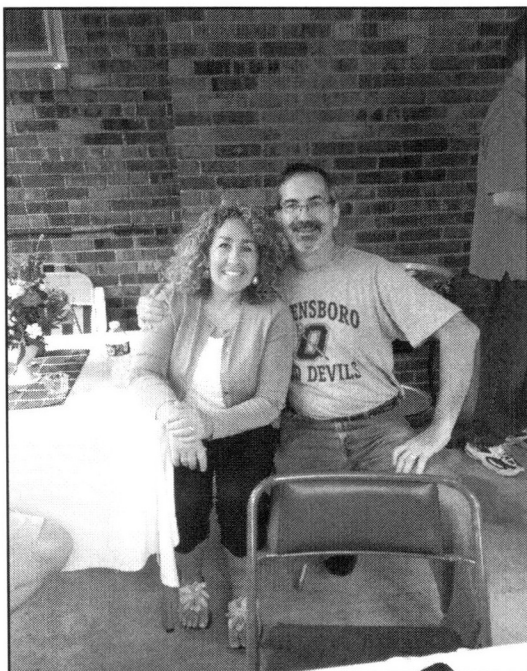

At one of our last Harrison family cookouts

Reconnecting with Old Friends

For some reason, during this grief, I decided to connect with people I had not seen or talked to in years. Maybe connecting with my past is a way to reset and discover who I'll be in this new life. I don't know. But one way I connected with old friends was through social media. That happened because I posted photos and stories about Ruth during my August tribute. Some of these old friends are male and some are female. Some had posted remarks to support Ruth and me during her battle and then to support me in my loss. Messaging them led to spending time with them on occasion. We would meet for a meal or go for a walk. One of those ladies has become a good friend. I enjoy spending time with her. That relationship has been another answer to prayer for relief from the emotional loneliness.

Grief Support Group

Though I was not very keen on the idea at first, I decided to attend a four-week grief group sponsored by the local hospice organization (Hospice and Palliative Care of Western Kentucky). Everyone in the group had lost their spouse. I was pleasantly surprised. It was helpful, listening to other grieved spouses talk about their situations. I consider the hospice grief coordinator, Caleb Potter, a friend now. He's been an ongoing source of help. I appreciate the fellowship there. And since attending that group,

I've learned that some local funeral homes also sponsor grief groups and meetings.

Tuning In to Music

After weeks of nothing holding my interest, and when sadness ruled the day, I allowed music back into my life. Like reconnecting with old friends, listening to some music and artists I enjoyed long ago refreshed me. I began relistening to my favorites from the '60s and '70s eras. I dug deeper by obtaining songs from beloved artists I hadn't heard before. Apps like Spotify make listening to artists, songs, and albums from any genre or era easy.

I was also blessed to learn of Christian songs that were recommended to me by my church family—songs by artists I was not familiar with before but who've become instrumental in my time of grief. I began listening to music during walks, runs, and bike rides.

For the first couple of months, music helped me pass the time without feeling so distraught. However, a couple of months later, the benefits of listening to music became apparent. I'm hesitant to say it brought me "joy" or "happiness," but I enjoyed some songs to the point that it distracted me from my grief. The emotion within music and the power of music to affect my emotions helped occupy my mind, giving me a temporary boost. Sometimes, the lyrics and music would bring tears to my eyes, as I thought of Ruth. Other times, conversely, it sparked happy thoughts of times we spent together. I now believe that whether listening to music kindles sadness or good memories, it helps me work through and process grief.

Another old friend I uncovered is my piano. This instrument is the same one I took lessons on as a child. I started practicing my piano skills by sight-reading hymns in our denomination's hymnal. I would play through two to six hymns daily to work on my skill and exercise my brain.

Another familiar musical activity I've returned to is composition. As a worship leader, music teacher, and choral director, writing music brought me great joy and fulfillment. With my newfound gloom, I wondered if I would ever write again. At about seven months into my loss, I was finally able to pen the words and melody to a song I would sing to Ruth if I could. I hope to release it online for the world to hear. The song is about my feelings for her, missing her, and trusting the Lord to carry me through the difficulty. This song, "Without You," was the first of several to stream into my mind.

I was inspired to compose like never before for a couple of months. Idea after idea would pop into my head. I could barely get anything else done because I frequently had to stop to write down ideas. Those thoughts have slowed, perhaps due to my progress, the arrival of summertime weather, outdoor work, and other activities. Still, it's one way God has been answering prayer. It was a special, fulfilling season. I even shared some of my tunes with friends and purchased new equipment and software to aid in composition and for fun. There's been little progress on that front, but there's so much to learn, and it's all new to me. Now, there's no shortage of things to do and discover.

Engaging in Service

Serving is something I believe I'll do more of as I continue to reengage in the ministries of my church. At this point, I have not resumed all the activities I did before, but I'm slowly getting back into it. I've also taken a more direct approach to helping the homeless in our area by increasing donations to local shelters, growing some food to donate to them, and preparing care packages of food and personal items to hand out to people asking for help on the street. I've also decided that, when confronted by a homeless person directly, I will go with the person to get them something they need. I've been able to do that on several occasions.

Living by This Theme

Somewhere along the line I realized I should be doing two things—celebrating the life I had with Ruth and growing where God has planted me now. These are reasons to live and enjoy the rest of my life. God hasn't finished using me yet, and he's not finished with you, either. Though not knowing the details of his plan is uncomfortable, I trust him. My wife was determined to enjoy life, no matter what. People who knew her tell me Ruth would insist I enjoy life too. I can hear her saying, "Life is too short. Go enjoy it." Easier said than done. But I'm working on it.

I have determined to take care of myself, learn, celebrate, and share. If life is to continue, even though I don't have all the answers, I must *take care of myself* physically, mentally, and spiritually. I should continue to *learn* new things—recipes, music, technology, and different ways to serve others. I need to *celebrate* the gifts I've been blessed with, not the least of which is my wife and the nearly thirty-five years we spent together. We shared a strong, unusual bond, and I'm celebrating that by writing this book. I also need to celebrate each new day, because that is the example Ruth set for me. I want to *share* things—my faith, feelings, music, and the lessons I've learned. And for anyone who will listen, I want to spread the word about that wonderful woman, Ruth Harrison, who completed me.

On a plane to Spain

In Summary

The first year without my wife has been hard—very hard. There's no denying that. But there have been positive points, as well. There's been progress. My faith has grown. I have endured, and God has proven faithful. I know I have a long way to go, but I have hope because he is with me. He's blessed me in the past and he's blessing me even during these trying days. I've been reminded that I can still use my gifts in a fulfilling way to bring joy to others.

There's more to my story; I just don't know how it will play out. That's very uncomfortable for me. In reality, it's simply playing out in a way I didn't have in mind. When you think about it, however, isn't that the way every life is in some way? If I ever needed proof that I'm not in charge, I have it now. I still cry sometimes, though not as often. I'm still extremely lonely at times. I still long for the wife I lost. I still miss Ruth as much as I did the first month she was gone. I'm still working through how to live without her. There is still the occasional sense that she can't be gone.

So what's a person to do? I realize other people may successfully process their grief differently than I do. Still, I would advise anyone who has lost their spouse to at least do these things:

Keep Moving

By "keep moving," I mean in multiple ways. One is physical activity. Regular exercise is very helpful to the body and mind. I walk, jog, and ride my bike.

One should also seek to engage in a project, pastime, or healthy degree of "busyness" to occupy the mind so as not to dwell constantly on one's loved one. Some of that time would be well spent doing things for others, especially those in need. Those types of actions have been helpful and fulfilling for me.

Reach Out

You need time alone to dwell on your loved one, but as you consciously allow yourself time to do that, also intentionally reach out to others to share time and thoughts. Don't stay home alone all the time. You need people, whether it be old friends, new friends, professional counselors, or church members. Some of them may have gone through what we have gone through. Since I used to be part of a couple, I try to remember that some of our couple friends are also grieving the loss of Ruth and can benefit from sharing grief with me.

Be Part of a Faith Community

Being part of a faith community was so helpful for me in my grief because I had already built relationships with people in my church. As life continues for a widow or widower, comfort, emotional support, and physical help can be found within a loving church family, which can keep one afloat. God blesses us in this way if we will partake. Sharing a like faith with others creates a sense of belonging that helps keep one grounded even in the midst of turmoil.

Journal

Keep track of what's going on and how you feel. A journal entry will inform and reward you when you return to review it.

Get into God's Word

The Bible "is a lamp for my feet, a light on my path" (Psalm 119:105). But I won't benefit unless I spend time reading and dwelling on it. There's practical help in God's Word—useful wisdom for every situation. Find a consistent time each day to devote to reading it. Memorizing Scripture has, in itself, power to comfort and strengthen. The Psalms have always been precious to me. But during this first year of my greatest loss, they have become more special than ever before. Many of them pour out the same emotions I have felt in my grief. They also help me to put things into perspective. One of the greatest attributes of the Bible is that it is the Word of God, an open window to him—an introduction to the One who has the power to help the most.

This grief is a journey. During the journey, we should not allow anyone to hurry us along. It's okay to go at your own pace. If you are walking a journey of grief, as I have been, it may be long and difficult, but you are not alone. Many have gone before us, and many are walking that road with us even now. Someone once said, "The degree of your grief shows how deeply you loved." A poem by Jamie Anderson states, "Grief is just love with no place to go." Those seem like good descriptions to me. My first year alone is in the books, but God willing, more blessings are on the way. So on to year number two.

I remain confident of this: I will see the goodness of the Lord in the land of the living. Wait for the Lord; be strong and take heart and wait for the Lord.
Psalm 27:13–14

About the Author

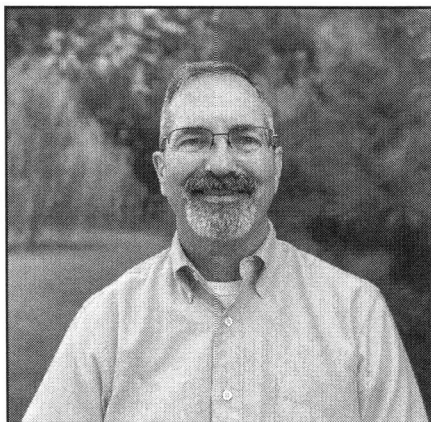

Vic Harrison is a retired National Board Certified teacher and worship leader. He was the music specialist at Sutton Elementary School in Owensboro, Kentucky, for over twenty years. Vic led worship in more than twenty-five churches and denominational settings around Kentucky and worked as a full-time music minister in Springfield and Burlington. He now lives in western Kentucky, where he and his late wife Ruth purchased land and built a home in 2016.

Just Me Now

Review Request

Thank you for reading *Just Me Now*. I hope it was helpful and encouraging. Your feedback is appreciated. Please take a moment to leave an honest review on Amazon or Goodreads. Doing so will help others discover this book. May God comfort you through loss and bless you for comforting others.

Made in the USA
Columbia, SC
30 November 2024